CAPE

IN OLDEN DAYS

Vintage Postcards of Gloucester, Rockport, & Environs

NANCY HELINSKI

TEXT BY PERRY MCINTOSH

Commonwealth Editions
Beverly, Massachusetts

ISBN-13: 978-1-933212-90-6

Front cover: Dog Bar Breakwater and Eastern Point Light, Gloucester

Designed by John Barnett/4 Eyes Design

Printed in Korea

Commonwealth Editions is the trade imprint of Memoirs Unlimited, Inc.,
266 Cabot Street, Beverly, Massachusetts 01915. Visit us on the Web at
www.commonwealtheditions.com.

The picture postcards in this book are part of my collection from around the world, a personal treasure I started assembling more than fifty years ago. I have always loved images of Cape Ann, the scene of many happy childhood memories. Our family cruised from Danversport through the Annisquam River to Wingaersheek Beach in my dad's motorboat, the *Jancy II*. We dined at restaurants along the Gloucester waterfront and docked alongside Motif #1 in Rockport. Our family celebrated the Fourth of July with a bonfire on the beach at Manchester, and in later years, I have enjoyed spending the day with family at Stage Fort Park, Good Harbor Beach, and Hammond Castle in Magnolia for organ concerts.

These older postcards of Cape Ann show many of the same spots and destinations that I loved as a child and that visitors flock to today. I am happy to share them with you, and I hope you enjoy them as much as I do.

Nancy Helinski

MURRAY GILMAN HOUSE

Gloucester

The Sargent-Murray-Gilman-Hough House at 49 Middle Street in Gloucester was built by Winthrop Sargent for his daughter Judith. A fine example of a merchant's house of the late eighteenth century, it is now a museum. Sargent supported the new Independent Christian Church in Gloucester and refused to pay taxes to the First Parish Church, prompting a lawsuit that helped establish religious freedom in Massachusetts.

MURRAY GILMAN HOUSE, GLOUCESTER, MASS.   106806

THACHER ISLAND

Rockport

B uilt in 1771, Thacher Island's twin lights were the last lighthouses built by
the British in the colonial era. The original towers, 45 feet tall, were replaced
in 1861 by 124-foot granite towers. Also in this view are the keeper's house,
the fog signal building, the oil house, and an old naval station. Today, Thacher
(frequently spelled *Thatcher* or *Thatcher's*) has the only operating twin lights on
the east coast of the United States.

Thatcher Light, Thatcher's Island of Cape Ann. Mass.

SINGING BEACH
Manchester

S inging Beach in Manchester (officially "Manchester-by-the-Sea") is one of only a few places in the world where beach sand makes a singing or squeaking sound when the wind blows over it or when it is stepped on. Scientists have no final explanation for this phenomenon.

BREAKING WAVES, SINGING BEACH, MANCHESTER-BY-THE-SEA, MASS.

HARBOR SCENE
Gloucester

Gloucester has always been a working port, and its waterfront has the gritty quality of a factory town. Some of the halibut caught off Gloucester was sold fresh, but much of it was smoked by being hung for several days in smokehouses fired by burning wood chips. Here white sails billow in front of smokestacks required for the fish drying, as well as for boatbuilding and other industries of a seaport city.

HARBOR SCENE, GLOUCESTER, MASS.   1176

OAKES' COVE, ROCKY NECK

Gloucester

A well-dressed man, probably a summer resident, keeps his feet dry as he draws his dinghy up on shore at Rocky Neck, a center for shipbuilding as well as a mecca for artists.

Oakes' Cove, Rocky Neck. GLOUCESTER, Mass.

THE BREAKERS, STRAITSMOUTH ISLAND

Rockport

The Straitsmouth Inn on Straitsmouth Island in Rockport harbor boasted several residences where families could spend the summer. The first summer homes known as "cottages" on Cape Ann were actually quite large houses where the wealthy from New York and Boston escaped the heat of the city summer. The first were built in the middle of the nineteenth century. According to Benjamin D. Hill, writing in 1880, "The majority of summer residences here are people of means and culture from Boston, New York, Philadelphia, and elsewhere, who have built fine residences and ornamented their grounds with great skill and taste. The place has always been noted as the summer rendezvous of people of literary and artistic taste." (*The North Shore of Massachusetts Bay*)

THE BREAKERS—One of the Straitsmouth Inn Cottages.

COLONIAL ARMS, EASTERN POINT
Gloucester

Built in 1904, the Colonial Arms boasted seventy-five rooms with private baths. "All sleeping apartments have an unobstructed water view and intercommunicating telephone connection." The hotel offered golf, yachting, tennis, bathing, and automobiling, and it had its own orchestra. The Colonial Arms was destroyed by fire in 1908.

13308— Colonial Arms Eastern Point, Gloucester, Mass. Why dont Mr Bond you take the car some fine morning ba Gloucester Th G. B

"OLD MOTHER ANN," EASTERN POINT

Gloucester

Many people see the shape of an old woman in this granite outcropping next to Eastern Point Light in East Gloucester. "Mother Ann rises to welcome you. Her chin is a bit grim, her nose decidedly austere, but there is great intelligence in her high brow, and a suggestion of warmth and repose in her big motherly form. The more you know her the more you will admire this noncommittal dame who guards the approach to her home." (*New York Times*, July 23, 1916)

G 7154 "Old Mother Ann", Eastern Point, Cape Ann, Mass.

O.K. G.E.O.

THE GULLEY, STRAITSMOUTH INN

Rockport

To an ordinary July observer the principal productions of this portion of Cape Ann seem to be rocks and roses," wrote Edwin P. Whipple, a nineteenth-century admirer. Visitors to Straitsmouth Island might have scrambled over this spot and listened to the roar of the incoming tide as it rushed through the narrow channel.

THE GULLEY

STRAITSMOUTH INN, ROCKPORT, MASS.

FISHERMEN'S MEMORIAL BY LEONARD CRASKE

Gloucester

This famous statue memorializes the Gloucester fishermen who have lost their lives at sea. The names of more than five thousand are immortalized on bronze plaques around the base of the statue. The quotation is from Psalm 107:

> THEY THAT GO DOWN TO THE SEA IN SHIPS, / THAT DO BUSINESS IN GREAT WATERS; / THESE SEE THE WORKS OF THE LORD, / AND HIS WONDERS IN THE DEEP.

THEY THAT GO
DOWN TO THE SEA
IN SHIPS
1623 ~ 1923

FISHERMAN'S MEMORIAL, Gloucester, Mass.

STRAITSMOUTH INN

Rockport

L yng about sixteen hundred feet offshore, Straitsmouth Island is one of the three "Turks' Heads." The other two are Thacher and Milk islands. This spacious inn on the island was recommended in the 1917 *Automobile Blue Book*.

63082　　　THE STRAITSMOUTH INN, ROCKPORT, MASS.

ANNISQUAM YACHT CLUB

Gloucester

Founded in 1896, the Annisquam Yacht Club is among the oldest in America. Annisquam was noted for its summer settlement of "Cambridge people."

ANNISQUAM YACHT CLUB, GLOUCESTER, MASS.

HISTORICAL SOCIETY

Manchester

B uilt as the residence of Capt. Richard Trask and his wife Abigail, married in 1823, this stately building stands on Union Street in the center of Manchester. As befits a historical society, the building features a collection of furniture manufactured near Manchester and photographs of summer homes in the vicinity.

HISTORICAL SOCIETY, MANCHESTER, MASSACHUSETTS   6987

MARMION WAY

Rockport

G uesthouses look out over calm seas and the beach on Marmion Way at
Gap Cove in Rockport.

A 6720 The Bay and Shore from Marmion Way, Rockport, Mass.

HARBOR ENTRANCE

Manchester

What is now Manchester-by-the-Sea was included in King Charles I's 1629 grant to the Massachusetts Bay Colony. In June of that year, the *Talbot* dropped anchor in the harbor, one of the best protected in Massachusetts Bay, and deposited settlers here. In 1845 a new period opened when the first summer resident built his vacation home here, and Manchester quickly became a fashionable watering place for wealthy city people.

Marshes, Brier Neck

Gloucester

Marshes cover much of Cape Ann, providing habitat for birds and other wildlife. The Great Marsh extends west and north from Gloucester, through the towns of Essex, Ipswich, Rowley, Newbury, Newburyport, and Salisbury.

FRESH MARSHES ALONG STATE HIGHWAY, BRIAR NECK, GLOUCESTER, MASS.

28990

THE PINES

Manchester

P ine forests were a common feature on Cape Ann. Modern-day hikers can still find quiet paths through tall trees and fields of glacial erratics (boulders pushed and left behind by glaciers of the last ice age). One popular walking spot is Ravenswood Park in Gloucester near the Manchester town line.

TEN POUND ISLAND LIGHT

Gloucester

The first light on Ten Pound Island was built in 1820 to improve navigation into Gloucester's inner harbor and to help sailors avoid a dangerous ledge near the island. The structure seen in this postcard was built in 1881.

TEN POUND ISLAND LIGHT, GLOUCESTER, MASS.

123442

THE HERMIT

Gloucester

Mason A. Walton moved to the pinewoods of Ravenswood in 1884 to improve his health. He lived here for thirty-three years. According to the *Gloucester Daily Times*, about four thousand visitors a year enjoyed the "agreeable and cultured conversationalist." Walton became a popular writer who signed his pieces "The Hermit," the name Gloucester townspeople had given him. The *Boston Globe* referred to him in a feature story as "one of the best known recluses in New England, if not the country."

Gloucester, Mass. -
The Hermit

STAGE FORT PARK
Gloucester

The plaque on this fifty-foot boulder in Stage Fort Park commemorates the Dorchester Company. This group of men from Dorchester, England, landed here in 1623 and set up a fishing camp, making Gloucester the first settlement in the Massachusetts Bay Colony. (The Plymouth Colony, famously settled in 1620, was a separate political entity at that time.) The plaque commemorates a settlement that was ultimately unsuccessful. A second, successful band of settlers arrived a few years later, and Gloucester was incorporated in 1642.

Rafe's Chasm

Magnolia

The almost perpendicular sides of this crevasse are 200 feet long and 60 feet deep, but Rafe's Chasm is only about 10 feet across. During storms, water rushes into the channel, shooting upwards with great force. A popular tourist spot during the nineteenth century, the chasm is now on private land and best seen by boat. It is maintained by The Trustees of Reservations.

181 RAFES CHASM, MAGNOLIA, MASS.

OLD STONE WHARFS

Annisquam

S tone quarried in Rockport was used to build wharves that have stood up to time and tide.

THE OLD STONE WHARFS, ANNISQUAM, GLOUCESTER, MASS.

HARBOR VIEW & TEN POUND ISLAND LIGHT

Gloucester

There are two popular stories explaining the origin of the name of Ten Pound Island. One holds that English settlers paid the Indians the sum of ten pounds for this spot in the middle of Gloucester Harbor. In the second version, "ten pounds" refers to ten paddocks holding sheep that settlers grazed there.

HARBOR VIEW AND TEN POUND ISLAND LIGHT, GLOUCESTER, MASS.

MANCHESTER HARBOR

Manchester

According to Benjamin D. Hill and Winfield S. Nevins, authors of *The North Shore of Massachusetts Bay*, a guide for tourists in 1880, "Manchester-by-the-Sea is one of the most attractive sea-shore resorts on the Atlantic Coast. It extends along the shore some four miles, presenting from the sea a picturesque front, a charming alternation of cragged rocks, forming bold headlands, and sandy beaches and inlets."

Mass., Manchester Harbor.

HARBOR SCENE

Gloucester

An idealized scene of tidy wharves, trim ships, and water as smooth as glass belies the danger and gritty reality of the fishing life.

HARBOR SCENE, GLOUCESTER, MASS.

SACRED HEART CHURCH
Manchester

Manchester's Roman Catholic parish was founded in 1905, and the first Mass was said in this church in May 1908.

SACRED HEART CHURCH, MANCHESTER, MASSACHUSETTS 5410

ROCKAWAY HOTEL
East Gloucester

One of many popular resort hotels of the late nineteenth century and early twentieth century, the Rockaway enjoyed a prime location on the beach at East Gloucester.

THE ROCKAWAY HOTEL, EAST GLOUCESTER, MASS.

123452

THE WILLOWS
Annisquam

The road shears the edge of a little meadow, cuts a belt of woods, which from the forest of the Cape's interior extends to the ocean's strand, and at the same point passes through a long beautiful arch of willows. This arch is the admiration and joy of the hundreds who every summer pass through it and enjoy its shade." (Henry C. Leonard, *Pigeon Cove and Vicinity*, 1873)

THE WILLOWS, ANNISQUAM, MASS.

ANNISQUAM YACHT CLUB

Annisquam

The *New York Times* of July 26, 1914, noted in an article entitled "Cape Ann Resorts: Hot weather fails to halt summer gaieties there," that "Notwithstanding the torrid weather, when the thermometer went up to 103 degrees at midday, there has been no diminution of outdoor activities. Boat racing, which holds the banner this year in open air sports, golf and tennis tournaments keep the Summer visitors on Cape Ann busy from early morn till dewy eve. . . . The yacht races of the Annisquam Yacht Club continue to be the centre of social interest at that resort."

THE YACHT CLUB, ANNISQUAM, GLOUCESTER, MASS.

WITCH HOUSE

Pigeon Cove

Any Pigeon Cove resident will direct you to what is known as the 'Witch House,' at your left as you follow Granite Street. So secluded is it still, almost smothered in trees and vines, and set back from the street at the end of a winding lane, that one can easily believe the tale of the two brothers who fled to this remote cape with their mother to save her from being persecuted as a witch. It is said that she was a victim of the Salem witchcraft mania, and was in danger of losing her life, when these devoted sons set about rescuing her. No authentic records exist, but there is a tradition that the name was Proctor." (*New York Times*, July 23, 1916)

THE OLD WITCH HOUSE, PIGEON COVE, MASS.

ANNISQUAM LIGHT

Annisquam

B uilt in 1801 to mark the entrance to the Annisquam River at Wigwam Point, the original wooden lighthouse was replaced with a brick tower in 1897. In 1931 a fog horn was added, but the signal operated only from October 15 through May 15 so that summer residents could enjoy the peace and quiet they had come to Annisquam to find.

ANNISQUAM LIGHT, GLOUCESTER, MASS.

WHALE'S JAW, DOGTOWN COMMON

Gloucester

The Whale's Jaw is one of several distinctive features of Dogtown, an abandoned inland settlement straddling Gloucester and Rockport that has long been a popular trekking spot for tourists and locals. Historian Joseph Garland quotes an old saying: "This being the last place created, all the rocks not needed in the rest of the earth were dumped here." On July 23, 1916, the *New York Times* noted, "The most famous of all the weird rocks is the 'Whale's Jaw,' but of the hundreds who send home a postcard with the jaw depicted thereon, not a tenth have ever penetrated to it and still fewer have wandered beyond." The lower part of the jaw was broken when a bonfire was set too close in the late twentieth century.

Gloucester, Mass. - Whales Jaw on Dogtown Common

FISHING BOATS

Gloucester

Picturesque fishing schooners filled Gloucester Harbor during the first half of the twentieth century. The last of the Gloucester-built Grand Banks fishing schooners was the *Gertrude L. Thebaud* (see p. 113), crafted at the Arthur D. Story yard in Essex in 1930.

FISHING BOATS IN PORT, GLOUCESTER, MASS.

123435

FISHING SCHOONER AND
S.S. CITY OF GLOUCESTER

Gloucester

The steamship *City of Gloucester* was 142 feet long. She plied the shores off Cape Ann, offering summer excursions for more than forty years around the turn of the twentieth century.

Fishing Schooner and S. S. "City of Gloucester," Gloucester, Mass.

MANCHESTER PUBLIC LIBRARY

Manchester

The cut-granite public library was a gift from T. Jefferson Coolidge, a prominent summer resident of Manchester. Charles Follen McKim, the prominent architect of the Boston Public Library, designed the building. It was dedicated in 1887.

A 7168 Public Library, Manchester-by-the-Sea, Mass

Charlie

WHEELER HOUSE

Gloucester

In the early twentieth century, Wheeler's Point, overlooking the Annisquam River and Ipswich Bay beyond, was the site of summer cottages for middle class people.

THE WHEELER HOUSE, WHEELERS POINT, GLOUCESTER, MASS.

SANDY BAY BEACH

Rockport

The *New York Times* described the scene in 1916: "You will pass charming summer homes, a beach where babies are toiling like ants to fill their sand-pails." Rockport was first known as Sandy Bay; fishermen from Ipswich and Essex came here seasonally in the 1600s to catch and dry fish. Sandy Bay Beach is now called Front Beach.

SANDY BAY BEACH, ROCKPORT, MASS.

ROCKY NECK COVE

East Gloucester

The painter Fitz Henry Lane was among the first of many artists to paint Cape Ann while visiting Rocky Neck, America's oldest art colony. Others have included Winslow Homer, Childe Hassam, Maurice Prendergast, Emile Gruppe, and Cecilia Beaux.

ROCKY NECK COVE, E. GLOUCESTER, MASS.

HARBOR COVE

Gloucester

In 1606, Samuel de Champlain discovered Gloucester and named the area in honor of its beautiful harbor and scenic coastline. In the account of his voyages, Champlain wrote, "This Harbor is very fine, containing water enough for vessels, and affording a shelter from the weather behind the islands. It is in latitude 43 degrees, and we gave it the name of Le Beauport."

VIEW IN HARBOR COVE, GLOUCESTER, MASS.

BREAKWATER, EASTERN POINT

Gloucester

The Dog Bar Reef was the site of many wrecks, and in 1866 fishing captain "Uncle Joe" Proctor petitioned Congress to build a breakwater to calm the waters of the outer harbor. The 2250-foot Dog Bar breakwater was built between 1894 and 1905 at a cost of $300,000; the light at its end marked the treacherous reef. According to lighthouse historian Jeremy D'Entremont, a severe storm in 1931 severed the cable to the breakwater lighthouse. The breakwater is now a favorite spot for angling.

BREAKWATER, EASTERN POINT, GLOUCESTER, MASS.

Annisquam Bridge

Annisquam

The bridge across Lobster Cove provided a short cut into the village of Annisquam from 1847 until it was closed to traffic in 1968. The wood-pile bridge, open now to pedestrians only, is in the National Register of Historic Places.

Copyrighted, 1905, by Martha H. Harvey.

Feb. 13, 1906

ANNISQUAM BRIDGE.

Compliments from
Mrs. W. L. Robinson.

VIEW OF PIGEON COVE

Pigeon Cove

Summer cottages line the shore at Pigeon Cove, part of Rockport. William Cullen Bryant wrote, "No place of resort by the sea-side in New England has such forest attractions as Pigeon Cove."

View of PIGEON COVE, Mass.

COMMON AND SQUARE

Rockport

Dock Square was the scene of the women's raid of 1856, a temperance march led by the hatchet-wielding Hannah Jumper. According to one eyewitness, "On finding any keg, jug, or cask having spirituous liquor in it . . . with their hatchets [they] broke or otherways destroyed it." No alcohol was sold in Rockport from that time until 2007, when the law was changed.

COMMON & SQUARE, ROCKPORT, MASS.

BLYNMAN BRIDGE

Gloucester

B uilt in 1906, the Blynman Bridge, or the "Cut Bridge," spans the canal connecting Gloucester harbor to the Annisquam River. The Reverend Richard Blynman supervised the work when the channel was first cut in the 1640s, providing fishing boats safe passage home from the north. Today it remains a very active drawbridge.

Gloucester, Mass. The Blynman Bridge.

MOORLAND AND COTTAGES

Bass Rocks

The Moorland was featured in the American Automobile Association's 1916 touring guide, *The Official Automobile Blue Book*. This useful publication included maps, points of interest, and perhaps most important, to facilitate route planning, the "character of roads." The circuit of Cape Ann was described as "a very beautiful trip," albeit on a dirt road in those days.

THE MOORLAND AND COTTAGES, BASS ROCKS, GLOUCESTER, MASS.

HAWTHORNE INN AND COTTAGES

East Gloucester

The "Social Notes" feature of the *New York Times*, July 29, 1910, informed readers that "W. Wetmore Cryder is in Boston after spending some weeks in town. Miss Mary Cryder has gone to the Hawthorne Inn, East Gloucester, Mass., where her father will join her in a few days." The Hawthorne was convenient to the Rocky Neck art colony.

The baby is 5 weeks old. He is named Alfred J.

Hawthorne Inn and Cottages, East Gloucester, Mass.

NORTHERN LIGHT

Thacher Island

Thacher Island was granted to John Thacher by the Massachusetts General Court in 1637, in compensation for having lost his family in a shipwreck here in the great storm of August 1635. The twin lights built on the island were the first to mark a dangerous spot on the coast; earlier lights merely indicated the mouths of harbors. The north light, seen here, was shut off in 1932 but is now relit as a private aid to navigation.

Thatchers Northern Light, near Gloucester, Mass.

ROAD BETWEEN MAGNOLIA & GLOUCESTER

The American Automobile Association's 1916 *Official Blue Book* describes Magnolia as "a summer resort on a rocky point projecting into the sea, with high cliffs on one side and Crescent Beach on the other; sometimes called 'the Newport of Massachusetts.'" According to this guide, the name of the town comes from wild magnolias that grew in nearby swamps, blossoms of which were sold by young boys in the street.

The Magnolia Road,
between Magnolia and Gloucester, Mass.

GEORGE A. PRIEST'S SCHOOL

Manchester

B uilt on Norwood Avenue in 1890, the George A. Priest School was razed in 1954.

George A. Priest School, MANCHESTER by the Sea, Mass.

OUR LADY OF GOOD VOYAGE

Gloucester

A t the end of the nineteenth century, immigrants from the Azores and
Portugal arrived in Gloucester in great numbers to work in the fishing
industry. They founded Our Lady of Good Voyage, a Roman Catholic church,
in 1889. The original painted wooden statue of the Madonna cradling a ship in
her arms can be seen in the Cape Ann Museum; a fiberglass replica now stands
atop the church. The Madonna is lighted at night to guide ships home.

THE PORTUGUESE CHURCH, LADY OF GOOD VOYAGE,

GLOUCESTER, MASS.

THE BEACHCROFT, EASTERN POINT

Gloucester

In 1917, the best room in the house in this resort opposite Niles Beach cost $38 a week, according to the *North Shore Blue Book* of that year.

The Beachcroft, Eastern Point, Gloucester, Mass.

WHITE ELLERY HOUSE

Gloucester

L ocated on Washington Street, the White Ellery House is a fine example of a first-period framed house in the saltbox style. Built in 1710, it is now a museum operated by the Cape Ann Historical Association.

The Old Ellery House, Gloucester, Mass.

This is the first one I've seen Jennie.

Made in Austria for W. G. Brown & Co., Gloucester, Mass. 56

HOTEL EDGECLIFFE, LONG BEACH

Rockport

I deally situated at water's edge between Brier Neck and Cape Hedge, the Hotel Edgecliffe looked out over the three Turks' Heads: Thacher, Straitsmouth, and Milk islands.

A 7161 Hotel Edgecliffe, Long Beach, Cape Ann, Mass.

Just for the day.

Minnie J. Spence.

ARTISTS' ROW, BEARSKIN NECK

Rockport

R ockport has been a favorite for artists—and art lovers—since the middle of the nineteenth century. Bearskin Neck was supposedly named by early fishermen for a bearskin laid there to dry by early settler John Babson. It was crowded with fishermen's shanties and bait shops until the middle of the twentieth century. It is now a popular tourist spot for art, souvenirs, and snacks.

ARTISTS' ROW, BEARSKIN NECK   ROCKPORT, MASS.

SCHOONER *GERTRUDE L. THEBAUD*

Gloucester

The *Gertrude L. Thebaud*, last of the Gloucester-built Grand Banks fishing schooners, was launched in 1930 with the express purpose of capturing the International Fisherman's Trophy from the Nova Scotia fleet. It sailed in two trophy series against Gloucester's archrival, *Bluenose*. In 1938, the Thebaud won two out of five races and finally took home the trophy. In April 1933 she carried a delegation to Washington, D.C., to plead on behalf of the hard-pressed fishing industry before President Franklin D. Roosevelt.

FISHING SCHOONER "GERTRUDE L. THEBAUD," GLOUCESTER, MASS.

SINGING BEACH
Manchester

The Singing beach is famous in the guide-books. Appleton makes mention of it; so have the tourist's letters for years. . . . The musical sound here will be noticed only when the sand is dry. When struck with the heel of the shoe or by an incoming wave it sends forth a peculiar musical sound." (Benjamin D. Hill and Winfield S. Nevins, *The North Shore of Massachusetts Bay*)

SINGING BEACH, MANCHESTER BY THE SEA, MASS.

DRYING FISH

Gloucester

The earliest settlers came to Gloucester to catch and dry fish to ship back to England and Europe. The members of the Dorchester Company set up fishing stages in what is now Stage Fort Park in 1623; they fished nearby waters for cod which were so abundant that explorer John Cabot declared a man could walk across the Grand Banks on their backs. In 1880, Benjamin D. Hill called Gloucester "the most extensive fishing port in the country if not in the world."

DRYING FISH, GLOUCESTER, MASS.

NILES BEACH

Gloucester

Niles Beach was named after Thomas Niles, who bought most of Eastern Point in 1844 and later won a court ruling that barred the public from most of the land. The Eastern Point Associates purchased the exclusive property in 1887, and in 1888 construction started on the first of eleven "cottages."

NILES BEACH, EAST GLOUCESTER, MASS.

EASTERN POINT LIGHT

Gloucester

Built in 1832, Eastern Point Light was first lighted in 1832. The new lighthouse's ten lamps showed a fixed white light fueled by whale oil. The first keeper was Samuel Wonson, hired at an annual salary of $400.

EASTERN POINT LIGHT FROM BREAKWATER, GLOUCESTER, MASS.

SQUAM ROCK

Annisquam

Coastal Massachusetts has many large glacial erratics, boulders deposited during the retreat of the last ice age. This immense stone is in Annisquam, in an area that is now heavily wooded.

SQUAM ROCK.   ANNISQUAM, MASS., ON CAPE ANN.   No. 44.

PUBLIC LIBRARY AND FIRST UNIVERSALIST CHURCH

Rockport

Universalism (the religion of John and Abigail Adams, Charles Bulfinch, and many other notable Americans) was considered by some in the early nineteenth century to be a "dangerous" doctrine. When the congregation of Universalists in Rockport was denied space in its earlier meeting house, the members built their own church in 1829, creating a classic New England village view.

PUBLIC LIBRARY AND FIRST UNIVERSALIST CHURCH, ROCKPORT, MASS.

ROCKPORT HARBOR

Rockport

Since the arrival of the first summer visitors, artists have set up their easels before Motif No. 1, this fisherman's shanty on Tuna Wharf. When the most painted and photographed building on Cape Ann was destroyed in the blizzard of 1978, the town rebuilt it to look exactly as it had before the storm, peeling paint and all.

11736. THE HARBOR, ROCKPORT, MASS.

EAGLE HEAD

Manchester

Winslow Homer spent time on Cape Ann and immortalized this view in his controversial 1870 painting "Eagle Head, Manchester, Massachusetts (High Tide)."

Eagle Head, Manchester, Mass.

Manchester Aug. 16, 1916.

THE TAVERN
Gloucester

Now a professional building, The Tavern overlooks the ocean from Stacey Boulevard near the public landing. The hotel was built in 1917.

THE TAVERN, GLOUCESTER, MASS.

GRANITE QUARRY

Rockport

Rockport granite is known for being clear and beautiful, without streaks or blemishes. According to a nineteenth-century observer, "There is hardly a city in the United States that has not some building, or monument, or street, built of Bay View Granite, while some of the finest Government buildings have been constructed wholly, or in part, from it." At the peak of the industry, Rockport quarries employed hundreds of men, but they largely shut down after the Great Depression.

A GRANITE QUARRY, ROCKPORT, MASS.

NORMAN'S WOE

Magnolia

A reef a short distance from the mainland, Norman's Woe is where the schooner *Hesperus* wrecked in the late seventeenth century. Essex County probate records show that the vessel and its master, Richard Norman, foundered here in 1680. Henry Wadsworth Longfellow immortalized the event in "The Wreck of the Hesperus":

> IT WAS THE SCHOONER HESPERUS, / THAT SAILED THE WINTRY SEA; /
> AND THE SKIPPER HAD TAKEN HIS LITTLE DAUGHTER, /
> TO BEAR HIM COMPANY.

Normans Woe, Magnolia, Mass.

STAGE COACH INN

Gloucester

Before the railroad came to Gloucester in 1847, visitors came up from Boston or New York by coach or carriage. The Stage Coach Inn's rustic, colonial-style building harkens back to that earlier time.

Stage Coach Inn
GLOUCESTER, MASS.

MOONLIGHT, GLOUCESTER HARBOR

Gloucester

G loucester Harbor can be tranquil. But let a southwest wind blow and this
picture would have many whitecaps.

Moonlight, Gloucester Harbor, Mass.

FISH HOUSES

Lanesville

Fishing shacks circled Lanesville Harbor, where day fishing in Ipswich Bay was a major occupation. The *New York Times* noted that "many of those [shacks] now huddled along the water's edge are of great age, and you will find many an old fisherman, as weatherbeaten and gray as his shingled dwelling, to tell you tales of early days." Lanesville was called Flatstone Cove until the Lane family settled here in the late 1600s. In the 1890s, about twelve hundred Finns settled in Lanesville, where the men found work in granite quarries.

Fish Houses, Lanesville, Mass.

GLOUCESTER HARBOR

Gloucester

While the fishing out of Gloucester is a far cry from the glory days of the nineteenth century, when schooners filled the harbor, several large firms, including the well-known Gorton's, continue to operate here in the twenty-first century.

3953—GLOUCESTER, MASS., FROM THE HARBOR.

Dear Philip,

I hope you will have a happy birthday and a pleasant time at your party! It is my birthday, too.

Your friend,

Edith W. Nickerson.

SOURCES FOR THE CAPTIONS:

Benjamin D. Hill and Winfield S. Nevins, *The North Shore of Massachusetts Bay, An Illustrated Guide and History of Marblehead, Salem, Peabody, Beverly, Manchester-by-the-Sea, Magnolia, and Cape Ann.* 3rd edition. Salem, 1880.

Jeremy D'Entremont, *The Lighthouses of Massachusetts.*

The *New York Times* archives online

The Official Automobile Blue Book of 1917, American Automobile Association.

The North Shore Blue Book and Social Register, 1917

Clifton Johnson, *New England, A Human Interest and Geographical Reader.* New York: Macmillan, 1857.

NANCY HELINSKI has been collecting picture postcards for over fifty years. Her extensive collection includes cards from all over the world. She is a native New Englander and now resides in Bradford, Massachusetts. This is her first book.

PERRY MCINTOSH is a writer and editor who lives in Salem, Massachusetts.